POINTS OF VIEW

Can POLICE REFORM Be Helpful?

By Layla Owens

KidHaven PUBLISHING

Published in 2023 by
KidHaven Publishing, an Imprint of Greenhaven Publishing, LLC
29 E. 21st Street
New York, NY 10010

Designer: Deanna Paternostro
Editor: Caitie McAneney

Photo credits: Cover Tomasz Warszewski/Shutterstock.com; p. 5 Debby Wong/Shutterstock.com; p. 7 Nic Neufeld/Shutterstock.com; p. 9 ALDECA studio/Shutterstock.com; pp. 11, 19 LightField Studios/Shutterstock.com; pp. 13, 21 (inset, middle) boyphare/Shutterstock.com; p. 15 Alexander Oganezov/Shutterstock.com; p. 17 Lutsenko_Oleksandr/Shutterstock.com; p. 21 (notepad) ESB Professional/Shutterstock.com; p. 21 (markers) Kucher Serhii/Shutterstock.com; p. 21 (photo frame) FARBAI/iStock/Thinkstock; p. 21 (inset, left) Jelani Photography/Shutterstock.com; p. 21 (inset, right) Jim Parkin/Shutterstock.com.

Library of Congress Cataloging-in-Publication Data

Names: Owens, Layla, author.
Title: Can police reform be helpful? / Layla Owens.
Description: New York : KidHaven Publishing, [2023] | Series: Points of view | Includes bibliographical references and index. | Audience: Grades 2-3
Identifiers: LCCN 2021047194 (print) | LCCN 2021047195 (ebook) | ISBN 9781534541870 (library binding) | ISBN 9781534541856 (paperback) | ISBN 9781534541863 (set) | ISBN 9781534541887 (ebook)
Subjects: LCSH: Police–United States–Juvenile literature. | Police administration–United States–Juvenile literature. | Police-community relations–United States–Juvenile literature.
Classification: LCC HV8139 .O94 2023 (print) | LCC HV8139 (ebook) | DDC 363.20973–dc23/eng/20211207
LC record available at https://lccn.loc.gov/2021047194
LC ebook record available at https://lccn.loc.gov/2021047195

Printed in the United States of America

CPSIA compliance information: Batch #CSKH23: For further information contact Greenhaven Publishing LLC, New York, New York at 1-844-317-7404.

CONTENTS

Call the Police! 4
Different Plans for Policing 6
Deadly Outcomes 8
High Risks 10
Changes to Training 12
Community Helpers 14
Accountability 16
Doing Their Jobs 18
Looking at Both Sides 20
Glossary 22
For More Information 23
Index 24

Call the POLICE!

Police reform, or change, is a very heated issue. In 2020, many people were upset about a police officer killing a Black man named George Floyd. They called for major changes to policing. Many said that police weren't helping communities of color, but instead were harming those communities. They said that police shouldn't be able to get away with **violence**.

Other people oppose police reform. They believe that police officers are necessary community helpers who do what they need to for public safety. They argue that police are necessary workers who need more support and funds, or money. They call the police heroes.

Know the Facts!

A 2020 Gallup poll showed that 58 percent of Americans believe changes to policing are necessary.

After George Floyd's death, many people took to the streets to **protest** against the police.

Different Plans for POLICING

People have different ideas of what police reform should look like. Some people want to abolish, or end, policing entirely. They would instead like to see a public safety system with nonviolent **emergency** helpers. They want all the money spent on policing to go toward health care, education, and community services—which they believe would stop crime.

Other people want to defund the police. That means cutting down large police **budgets** and using some of the money for social services. Still others want to reform policing through better training and holding police officers **accountable** for their actions.

Know the Facts!

In 2018, the Urban Institute found that state and local governments spend about 3.7 percent of their budget on police.

Police reform is a complex issue, which means it doesn't have one easy answer.

Deadly OUTCOMES

People who think police reform can be helpful often point out times when police were violent toward unarmed people. They argue that police shouldn't use deadly force or **weapons**, such as guns. Instead, they think that police should be trained to use non-deadly actions and weapons.

A study from Harvard University found that Black Americans were 3.23 times more likely to be killed by police than white Americans between 2013 and 2017. People argue that **racism** in policing isn't just unfair—it's deadly. They say police reform measures that combat, or fight, racism could help make communities safer for everyone.

Know the Facts!

The Mapping Police Violence database found that police killed 1,126 people in the United States in 2020.

Most killings by police are shootings. People want to reform policing to include non-deadly options for solving problems.

High RISKS

Many people who oppose police reform argue that police officers have high risks on the job. Their jobs take them into many life-and-death **situations**. People often call the police when faced with violent situations, such as another person with a gun. Having a gun can keep the police officer and others safe.

Many people argue that police need more tools and support, not less. They argue that police need to be armed with weapons and bulletproof clothing to survive, or stay alive. This is especially important to people who have a police officer in their family. They want their loved one to come home from work safe.

Know the Facts!

Between 2003 and 2014, an average of 115 police officers and sheriff's patrol officers died because of work injuries each year.

Police officers have friends and family who care about their safety in their high-risk job.

Changes to TRAINING

People who want police reform often want better training for police officers. This includes **diversity** training, which would teach police officers how to respect and understand people of different races and backgrounds. Trainings can help police recognize racism. Other kinds of training could help police know what to do if a person is having a **mental** health **crisis**.

Many people want police to have training in managing **conflict**. They would learn how to calm a situation before it turns violent. They could also have training to help them work on dealing with their feelings and **stress**.

Know the Facts!

The 2020 Gallup poll found 88 percent of Black Americans want changes to policing in the United States, compared to 51 percent of white Americans.

Some people argue that people of color are harmed by police officers more often than white people. Diversity training and other kinds of reforms could help stop what these people see as racism in policing.

Community HELPERS

People who oppose police reform argue that police are essential workers, or important to community life. They say police officers do much more to help than to harm.

People point to all the good that police officers already do in their communities. They help keep construction workers safe as they work on highways. They keep schools safe. They help kids who are lost. They work at parades and big community events to make sure everyone is safe. Some people say the news only shows what a few police officers do wrong and rarely shows what police do right.

Know the Facts!

The U.S. Department of Justice says that police and community members can build trust through ride-alongs with officers, police visits at schools, and taking part in peaceful marches.

Many people argue that the police have a community's best interests in mind. They think abolishing or defunding the police wouldn't help communities.

ACCOUNTABILITY

People often find out about unfair or violent police actions because of videos taken on cell phones and shared online. Now, many police officers are also made to wear body cameras to capture videos.

Some people argue that even when videos prove a police officer acted badly, they often still aren't held accountable. These people believe reforms are needed so police officers who act unfairly or break the law are punished. Many people believe that holding police officers accountable for their actions would make the people they deal with more likely to trust them.

Know the Facts!

From 2013 to 2020, more than 98 percent of killings by police did not result in officers being charged with a crime.

Police body cameras help record what happens when police and other people interact, or meet.

Doing Their JOBS

The reason why many police officers aren't held accountable is because of qualified immunity. Qualified immunity means that police officers are safe from being **sued** unless they act in a way that goes against someone's clearly known and established, or set, rights. This can be hard to prove.

Some say qualified immunity is necessary to help the police do their jobs. They argue that police officers shouldn't be punished for actions they took to keep the public safe. Police officers have to make many quick decisions. They often don't have time to second-guess their actions for fear of being sued.

Know the Facts!

The 1967 Supreme Court case *Pierson v. Ray* recognized the use of qualified immunity in court.

Many people argue that police officers need to be able to do their jobs without worrying about being sued.

Looking at BOTH SIDES

There are many arguments around police reform. Some people think that police officers shouldn't have to do so many tasks. For example, social workers can help with mental health calls. In this way, they argue, police reform could help both communities and police officers.

Other people think that police reform would not be helpful. They argue that police need all the funding they can get and do not need more stress on the job. Many people see a middle path in which police officers are better trained and supported. You've seen both sides of this debate. What's your point of view?

Know the Facts!

Some police officers in cities around the United States joined peaceful protests after George Floyd's death in 2020.

Can police reform be helpful?

YES

- Police reform can reduce the number of people killed by police by reducing or stopping officers' use of deadly force and weapons.
- Police need better training.
- When officers are held accountable, people are more likely to trust the police.
- Police have too many tasks.

NO

- Police need weapons for their high-risk jobs.
- Police do many good things in communities and do not need new rules and reforms.
- Police need to be able to do their job without worrying about being sued.
- Police need as much funding and support as possible.

Looking at both sides can help you make an educated decision.

GLOSSARY

accountable: Required to explain actions or choices.

budget: A plan for spending.

conflict: A fight.

crisis: A difficult and often unsafe situation that needs attention.

diversity: The quality or state of having many different types, forms, or ideas.

emergency: An unexpected and often unsafe situation that calls for immediate action.

mental: Dealing with the mind.

protest: To speak out strongly against something.

racism: The practice of treating others poorly because they are part of a different race, or group of people who look alike in certain ways.

situation: All the facts, conditions, and events that affect someone or something in a certain time and place.

stress: Something that causes strong feelings of worry.

sue: To bring a case against a person in court.

violence: The use of force to harm someone.

weapon: Something used to fight an enemy.

For More INFORMATION

WEBSITES

PBS Kids Talk About: Race & Racism
pbslearningmedia.org/resource/pbs-kids-talk-about-race-racism/pbs-kids-talk-about-race-and-racism-media-gallery/
"Racism" is a term often used in debates about police reform, and this video explains race and racism in a way that's easy for kids to understand.

Police Facts for Kids
kids.kiddle.co/Police
What do police officers do? Find out with this resource all about the police.

BOOKS

Bender, Douglas. *Police Officer*. St. Catharines, Ontario: Crabtree Publishing Company, 2022.

Markovics, Joyce L. *2020 Black Lives Matter Marches*. Ann Arbor, MI: Cherry Lake Publishing, 2021.

Roberts, Antonia. *Police Officers*. Minneapolis, MN: Bearport Publishing, 2021.

INDEX

A
accountability, 6, 16, 18, 21

B
body cameras, 16, 17
budgets, 6, 20

C
communities, 4, 6, 14, 15, 21

D
diversity training, 12

E
education, 6, 20

F
Floyd, George, 4, 5
funds, 4, 6, 20, 21

G
guns, 8, 10

M
mental health, 12, 20

P
protests, 5, 20

Q
qualified immunity, 18

R
racism, 8, 12
risks, 10, 11, 20, 21

S
social services, 6, 20
stress, 12, 20
Supreme Court, 18

T
tasks, 20, 21

U
U.S. Department of Justice, 14

V
videos, 16
violence, 4, 8, 10, 12, 16

W
work injuries, 10